Marie R

for

Lila

de

Nobili

MARY
Queen of Scots

Evocation
Roy Strong

Spectacle
Julia Trevelyan Oman

SECKER & WARBURG · LONDON

First published in England 1972 by
Martin Secker & Warburg Limited
14 Carlisle Street, London W1V 6NN

SBN 436 50021 3

Printed in England by Westerham Press Limited, Westerham, Kent

om Lady Day to Michaelmas a drum was beaten in the courtyard of the
rl of Shrewsbury's house at six in the morning. It signalled not only the
ginning of the day for his own household, but for that of the prisoner in
s charge. For fourteen years Lord Shrewsbury had in his custody the
iled Queen of Scots, a task in which he laboured long in 'the service of
izabeth of England who did little in return but scold the behaviour of one
ho was 'the keeper of so great a charge'. Within his houses of Wingfield,
heffield Castle and Sheffield Lodge, he and his Countess, the formidable
ess of Hardwick, gave room to a court in exile. A strange assemblage of
cots and French, together with native English servants recruited within
e locality, made up an entourage of some forty persons. The number
ictuated over the years as efforts were periodically made to reduce the
ueen of Scots' train and therefore the cost of keeping this great lady in
straint. The Queen had her own master of the household, physicians,
rgeon, and apothecary, her own reader and embroiderer, her own grooms
the chamber and tailors. There was a kitchen staff of eight, a coachman
id three grooms of the stable. In the round of her daily life her secretaries
d her gentlewomen of the chamber were closest to her of all.
Although her long years as a prisoner of the Queen of England were
imed by sojourns in other houses, Bolton, Tutbury, Chartley, Wingfield
d finally Fotheringhay, she lived fourteen out of the seventeen in two,
heffield Castle and Sheffield Lodge, broken only by occasional excursions
Chatsworth some three and a half hours' ride away. Mary was in
heffield Castle or Lodge from 28th November 1570 to 2nd September
84. Sheffield Lodge we know had a great gallery, a tower chamber, the
ieen's gallery, the Queen's chamber and her outer chamber. At Tutbury
e lodgings provided for her use were 'the chiefest of the house', a dining
amber thirty-six feet long, opening onto a 'fair cabinet private with a
imney'. This in turn led into her bedroom, twenty-seven feet long with
ace for two beds and a pallet with a 'proper closet private adjoining'.
ary's account of her accommodation was a very different one. She com-

plained that it was built only of plaster and wood and that the garden w
'fitter to keep pigs in than to bear the name of a garden'. 'I am in a wall
enclosure, on top of a hill,' she lamented, 'exposed to all the winds an
inclemencies of heaven.'

Everywhere she went during her imprisonment her court occupied
similar number of rooms. Two for herself, three for her maids, two f
wives of men in her service, eight for gentlemen officers and men servant
of whom two were her secretaries, one was her master of the househol
another her physician, and one more, her almoner or reader (who w
covertly a priest). All these had to have separate apartments. Within th
interconnecting nest of rooms the Queen of Scots' court created its ov
world and lived its own life governed by the dictates of its mistress. T
court existed in isolation, guarded on all sides by the soldiers and retaine
of successive gaolers. At Wingfield we hear of two hundred persons maki
up the household, a hundred and twenty of Lord Shrewsbury's servan
and fifty of Sir Ralph Sadler's, of whom forty were soldiers. These, arm
at all points, guarded the approaches to the Queen of Scots' rooms and
night stood beneath the windows of her lodging.

As the Queen was moved from house to house as a prisoner under arm
escort, her possessions travelled with her, so that her surroundin
remained remarkably consistent over the years. Although it was written
1584 that 'she hath no stuff of her own, neither hangings, bedding, pla
napery, kitchen vessels, nor anything else', except the worn and shab
items sent by Elizabeth, a different picture can be pierced together from t
various inventories of her possessions compiled over the years. There we
tapestry hangings, including the six pieces of the battle of Ravenna, t
history of Meleager, and the Labours of Hercules. There were Turk
carpets to place around her bed and beneath her feet in her dining-room
dais of violet velvet and a further travelling bed with a pavilion of bl
damask over it. Her rooms were lit with 'chaundellours' and there we
chairs of crimson velvet and cloth of gold. The Queen's maids sat
embroidered stools and she and her entourage ate off silver plate. Furnitu

ecame sadly worn over the years, and by 1585 her carpets were very
agged: 'She hath the best of the old long ends to walk on in her chamber,'
. was written, 'which is matted, but yet too hard for her sore foot. The
ining chamber floor is plaster, very cold, though strewed with rushes.'
Central to all was her maintenance of a privy and presence chamber as in a
oyal palace with its dais and cloth of estate beneath which she sat as Queen.

Throughout these long years Mary surrounded herself with portraits
ecalling happier days. There were ones of members of the French royal
amily, her brothers-in-law, Charles IX and Henry III, her sister-in-law,
Marguerite de Valois, her Guise relations, the Cardinal and Duke of
Guise, besides paintings of all the Kings of Scotland from James II down
o her son, James VI. Her jewels record other likenesses associated with
anished glories: Henry III and his queen, Louise of Lorraine, her first
usband, Francis II, her mother-in-law, Catherine de' Medici, and her
econd husband, Lord Darnley. An agate carried a picture of another
Catholic Queen, Mary Tudor, and a mirror decorated with silver bore the
aces of the Duchess of Savoy and of her mother, Mary of Guise.

The Queen of Scots' day was passed almost entirely amidst her own
eople, principally her gentlewomen. In her youth she had been served by
he celebrated four Maries, ladies of aristocratic Scottish birth sent to
France to wait on the infant Queen: Mary Beton, Mary Seton, Mary
Livingstone and Mary Fleming. Of these Mary Seton alone accompanied
er mistress into exile, serving her fifteen years until at last she withdrew to
convent close to Rheims. By 1586 Bastian Pagès, her favourite *valet de
chambre*, and the man upon whose wedding night her second husband Lord
Darnley was murdered, was apparently the only member of her household
dentifiable with the days of her rule in Scotland. In that year her gentlewomen were all recusant Catholic ladies, Jane Kennedy, Elizabeth and
Barbara Curle, Gillis Mowbray and a certain Mistress Beaugarde. Elizabeth
Curle withdrew to the Continent after her mistress' execution, living on
nto the next century to perpetuate the legend of the martyr Queen in the
xtraordinary portrait of Mary dressed as for her execution. There the two
adies who attended her on the scaffold, Jane Kennedy and Elizabeth Curle,
tand tearful in the background as the axe falls.

A considerable amount is known of Mary's personal appearance. A
fifteen her beauty had 'shone like the light at mid-day', her hazel eye
sparkled and her complexion was fresh and clear, 'very lusome' as Si
James Melville once described it. Mary had inherited from her mother th
tall stature of the Guise family which showed her to advantage on a
public occasions and in the exercise of the chase and of the dance. By 1569
when she was twenty-seven, Lord Shrewsbury was uncharitably to repor
to his mistress that the exiled Queen's 'colour and complexion . . . i
presently much decayed'. Fourteen years later, constantly beset by i
health and restrained from exercise in the fresh air, Robert Beale refers t
her as 'waxen far grosser than ever I saw her'. At her trial she struck an on
looker as 'high, bigg made, and somewhat round shouldered'. By then th
tall graceful sonnet mistress of the poets of the French court had becom
a plump middle-aged lady with a face 'full and flat, double chinned'. Ove
the years too her hair had gradually progressed from a ruddy yellow t
auburn, from auburn to dark brown or seemingly, to some eyes, black
Mary's hair turned grey long before its time and this she concealed b
cropping it and wearing a wig. One of the four Maries, Mary Seton, wa
hailed to be 'the finest dresser of a woman's head of hair that is to be see
in any country'. Every day during the period following her arrival int
England she decked out the Queen of Scots' head with some new and mor
'delicate' creation of false hair. When the executioner held up the roya
head on the scaffold he found himself holding the Queen's wig while he
head fell onto the boards beneath.

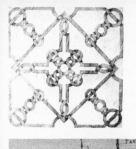

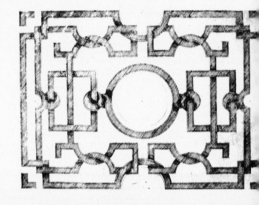

AMBOISE

FACIES LIGERIN SPECTANTES
FACES DV COSTE DE LA
RIVIERE DE LOIRE

The Armies of Marie Quene Dolphines of France,
The nobillest lady in earth for till advance ;
Of Scotland Quene, of Ingland also,
Of Ireland also God hath providit so.

. . . as her youth grew on, we saw her great
beauty and her great virtues grow likewise; so
that, coming to her fifteenth year, her beauty
shone like the light at mid-day . . . As long as
she lived in France she always reserved two
hours daily to study and read; so that there
was no human knowledge she could not talk
upon. Above all she loved poetry and poets . . .
She was a poet herself and composed verses,
of which I have seen some that were fine and
well done . . . Moreover she wrote well in
prose, especially letters, of which I have seen
many that were very fine and eloquent and
lofty. At all times when she talked with others
she used a most gentle, dainty, agreeable style
of speech, with kindly majesty, mingled, however, with discreet and modest reserve, and
above all with beautiful grace; so that even
her native tongue, which in itself is very rustic,
barbarous, ill-sounding, and uncouth, she
spoke so gracefully, toning it in such a way
that she made it seem beautiful and agreeable
in her, though never so in others.

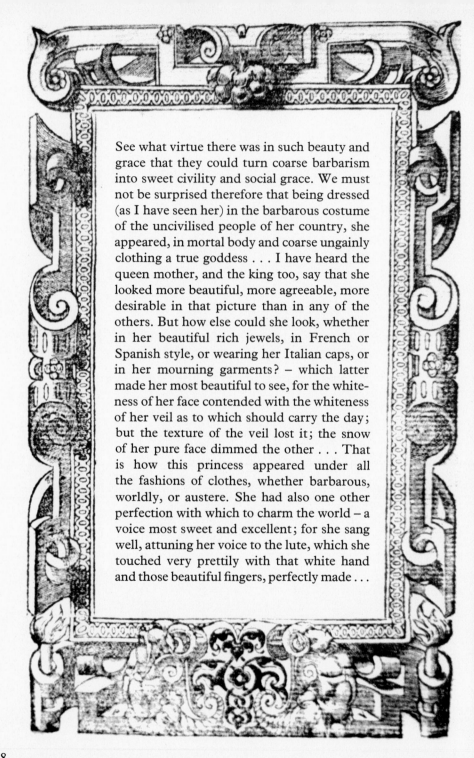

See what virtue there was in such beauty and grace that they could turn coarse barbarism into sweet civility and social grace. We must not be surprised therefore that being dressed (as I have seen her) in the barbarous costume of the uncivilised people of her country, she appeared, in mortal body and coarse ungainly clothing a true goddess . . . I have heard the queen mother, and the king too, say that she looked more beautiful, more agreeable, more desirable in that picture than in any of the others. But how else could she look, whether in her beautiful rich jewels, in French or Spanish style, or wearing her Italian caps, or in her mourning garments? – which latter made her most beautiful to see, for the whiteness of her face contended with the whiteness of her veil as to which should carry the day; but the texture of the veil lost it; the snow of her pure face dimmed the other . . . That is how this princess appeared under all the fashions of clothes, whether barbarous, worldly, or austere. She had also one other perfection with which to charm the world – a voice most sweet and excellent; for she sang well, attuning her voice to the lute, which she touched very prettily with that white hand and those beautiful fingers, perfectly made . . .

L'escossoise.

Si vous baissez l'œil dessus ce pourtrait
Pour bien sçauoir d'Escossoise la forme,
Cestuy cy est au naturel consorme,
Comme voyez qu'au vis il est pourtrait.

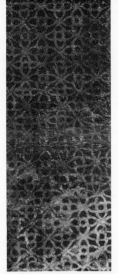

m ane claith of estate of grene veluot in the
*ilk thair is ane great trie/and personageis/
*d scheildis/all maid embroiderie/furnisit
*h thre pandis and the taill/all freinyeit with
*ne silk and threid of gold.

m ane bed of crammosie broun veluot/maid
broderie work and leiffis of claith of gold/
*h sum histories maid in the figure ovaill/
*nisit with ruif heidpece and sex pandis and
*e vnderpandis/all frenyeit with threid of
*d and crammosie silk . with thre curtenis of
*mmosie dames/pasmentit with gold/and
*nyeit with the same/and also foure
*eringis for the bed stowppis.

m ane bed of fresit claith of gold/with
*uchtes of reid silk/in figure of jennettis and
*sonageis and brancheis of holine/furnisit
*h ruif heidpece/thre single pandis twa
*derpandis/and all freinyet with threid of
*d and crammosy silk.

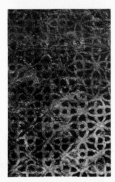

Il pensier che mi nuoce insieme e giova
Amaro e dolce al mio cor cangia spesso
E fra tema e speranza lo tien si oppresso
Che la quiete pace unque nó trova.

Pero, se questa carta à voi rinuova
Il bel disio di vederui in me impresso
Cio fa il grand'affanno ch'in me stesso
Ha, non puotendo homai da se far prova.

Ho veduto talhor vicino al porto
Rispinger naue in mar contrario vento
E nel maggior seren' turbarsi il Cielo

Cosi sorella chara temo e pauento
Non gia per noi, ma quante volte à torto
Rompe fortuna un ben'ordito uelle?

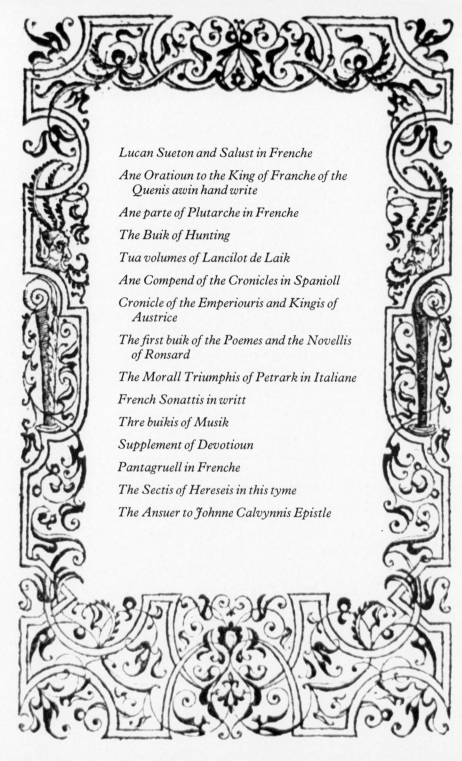

Lucan Sueton and Salust in Frenche

Ane Oratioun to the King of Franche of the Quenis awin hand write

Ane parte of Plutarche in Frenche

The Buik of Hunting

Tua volumes of Lancilot de Laik

Ane Compend of the Cronicles in Spanioll

Cronicle of the Emperiouris and Kingis of Austrice

The first buik of the Poemes and the Novellis of Ronsard

The Morall Triumphis of Petrark in Italiane

French Sonattis in writt

Thre buikis of Musik

Supplement of Devotioun

Pantagruell in Frenche

The Sectis of Hereseis in this tyme

The Ansuer to Johnne Calvynnis Epistle

MARIA IACOBI SCOTRVM REGIS FILIA,
SCOTORVMQVE NVNC REGINA

F H

Hans liefrinck excud

27

Inuentaire de tous les ahabillemens d'
Royne...

Vne robbe de toille dargent frisee do
dargent et trassee de soye cramoysy
bordee dung passement dor faict a bour

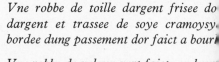

Vne robbe de veloux vert faicte en bour
toute couuerte de broderye ginpeure
cordon dor et dargent et bordee d'
passement de mesmes.

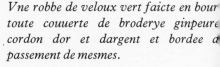

Vne robbe de satin bleu faicte a borletz t
couuerte de broderye en fasson de ross
feullages faictz dargent, et le reste cordo
dor et bordee dung passement dor.

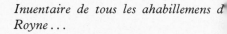

Item vne manteau royale de veloux vio

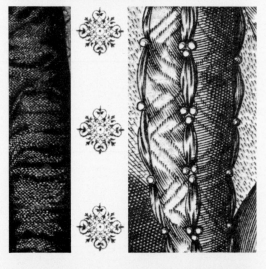

Vung manteau ront de taffetas gris fait
Espagnolle toute couuerte de broderye
petitz jazerant dargent et tout double
panne de soye blanche et borde dung gr
passement dargent.

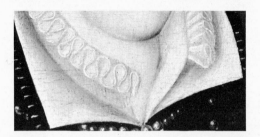

vasquine de toille dargent frisee le
s et bourletz figuree et frisee de rouge.

vasquyne de satin viollet chamaree par
les de broderye faicte par cheuron de
etille dargent bordee dung passement
ent.

deuant de cotte de satin cramoys tout
ert de broderye de petis cordons dor.

deuant de cotte de satin incarnat de
erye de ginpeure de plusieurs couleurs
asson de quannetille et cordon dor.
grand manteau royal garny de pare-
darmyne lentour de mesmes et le reste
le de taffetas blanc.

petit manteau de chambre faict de
x noyer enrechie dune bande de petite
dargent faict en fasson treffles.

Ce qui est au Cabinet de ladicte Dame.

Vng petit vaze de cristal de roche garny dor et enrichy de deux petites turquoises et de petis rubiz.

Vne petite cage dor ou il y a vng perroquet dedans.

Vng pigeon dor emaille de blanc et de noir.

Vne pomme dor facon Dinde garnye de petits rubiz taincts et de turquoises.

Vne enseigne facon de Serine garnie de diamant et dun rubiz qui sert a peigner.

Vne autre enseigne dun Cupido ou il y a vng petit rubiz au bout dune torche.

Vng lyon de nacque de perles garny dor.

Vng enseigne dor ou il y a vne femme qui chasse Cupido.

Vng petit mirouer de cristal garny dor.

Vng petit mouton dor esmaille de blanc.

Vne petite pomme dor ou il y a le feu Roy Descosse.

Vng petit chien dor esmaille de blanc et de noir.

Deux faueurs dune torche et dune lance.

Vne autre lance tournee dun roulleau garny de flambes de feu.

Deux langues de serpentz.

Quatre petitz panniers dor de fruictz.

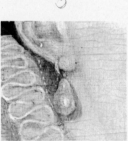
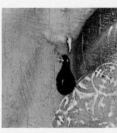

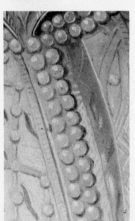

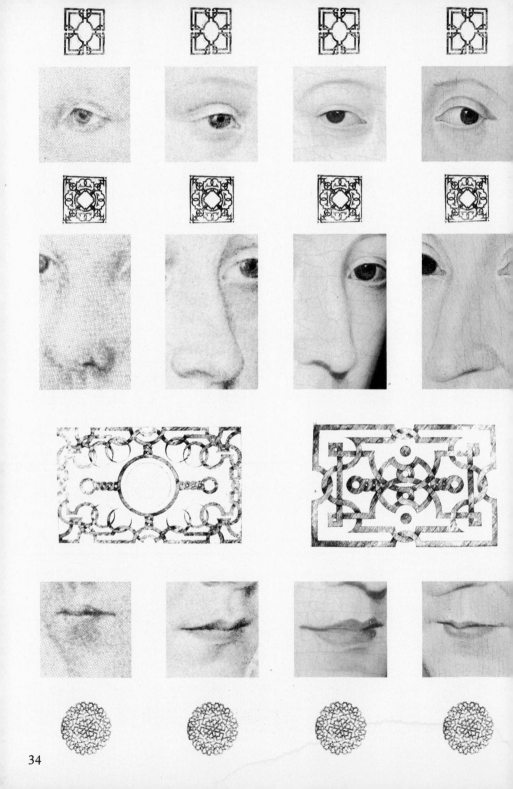

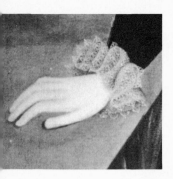

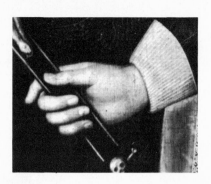

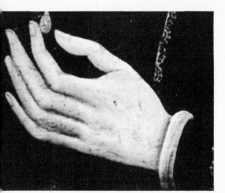
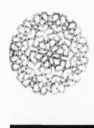

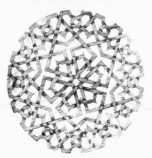

Her hair of itself is black, and yet Mr Knollys
told me that she wears hair of sondry colours.

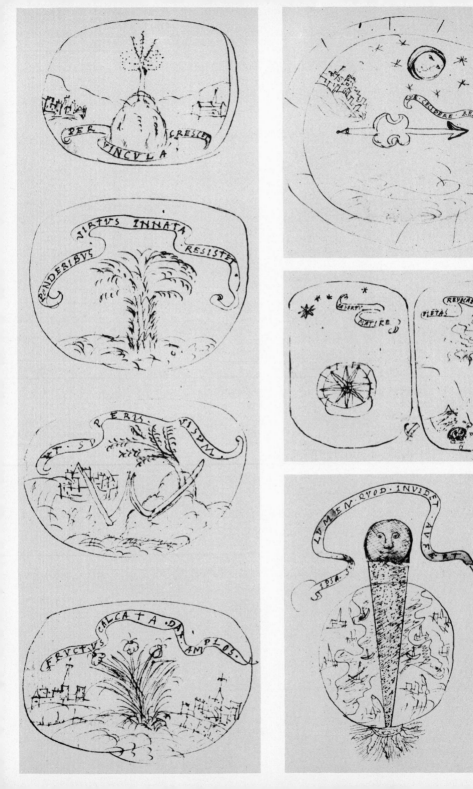

I have been curious to find out for you, the *Impressaes* and Emblemes on a Bed of State wrought and embroidered all with gold and silk by the late Queen Mary . . . which will embellish greatly some pages of your Book, and is worthy your remembrance.

MA= RIA.

Regina Scotia

She is a goodly personage . . . hath withall an alluring grace, a prety Scottishe accente, and a searching wit, clouded with myldness . . .

MARIA
D   G
SCOTIÆ
PIISSIMA REGINA
FRANCIÆ DOWERIA
ANNO
ÆTATIS REGNI
36
ANGLICÆ CAPTIVA
10
S   H
1578

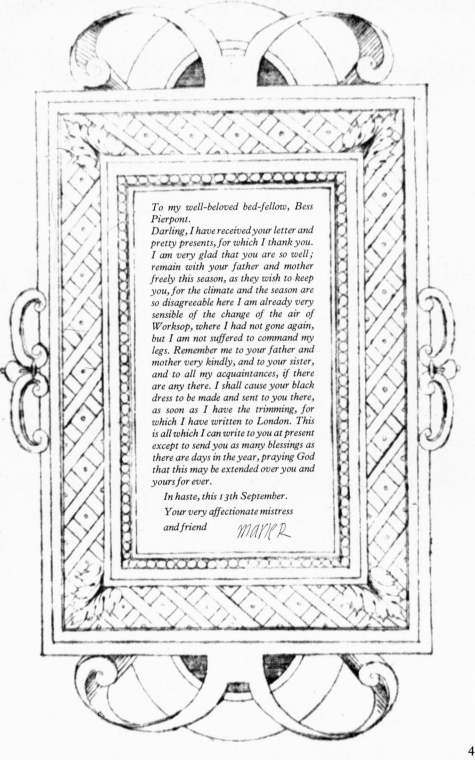

To my well-beloved bed-fellow, Bess Pierpont.

Darling, I have received your letter and pretty presents, for which I thank you. I am very glad that you are so well; remain with your father and mother freely this season, as they wish to keep you, for the climate and the season are so disagreeable here I am already very sensible of the change of the air of Worksop, where I had not gone again, but I am not suffered to command my legs. Remember me to your father and mother very kindly, and to your sister, and to all my acquaintances, if there are any there. I shall cause your black dress to be made and sent to you there, as soon as I have the trimming, for which I have written to London. This is all which I can write to you at present except to send you as many blessings as there are days in the year, praying God that this may be extended over you and yours for ever.

In haste, this 13th September.

Your very affectionate mistress
and friend   *Marie R*

I asked hir Grace, sence the wether did cutt off all exercises abrode, howe she passed the tyme within. She sayd that all that day she wrought with her nydill, and that the diversitie of the colors made the worke seme lesse tedious and contynued so long at it till veray payn made hir to give over . . .

I pray you procure for me some turtle-doves, and some Barbary fowls, to see if I can rear them in this country . . . I shall take great pleasure in bringing them up in a cage, as I do all the little birds that I am able to obtain. These are pastimes for a prisoner, and especially as there are none in this country.

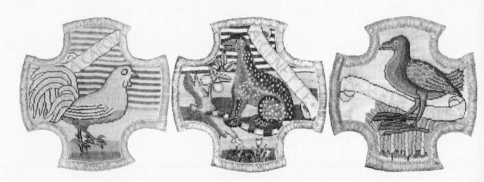

If my uncle, the Cardinal of Guise, has gone to Lyons, I am sure he will send me a couple of pretty little dogs, and you will buy me as many more; for except in reading and working, my only pleasure is in all the little animals I can get. They must be sent in baskets, well stored, so as to keep them warm.

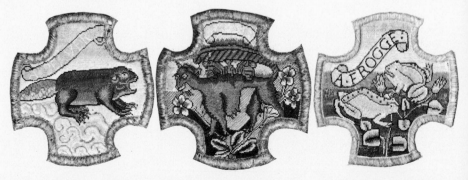

There are some of my friends in this country who ask for my portrait. I pray you, have four of them made, which must be set in gold, and sent to me secretly, as soon as possible.

Was ever known a fate more sad than mine?
 Ah! better death for me than life, I ween!
For me there is no sorrow's anodyne:
 T'wards me all change their nature and their mien.

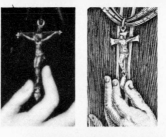

La croix d'or, gravée des Mysteres de la Passion

Grosses patenostres d'or et agathe en vases

La croix d'or que sa Majesté avoit accoustume
de porter

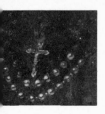

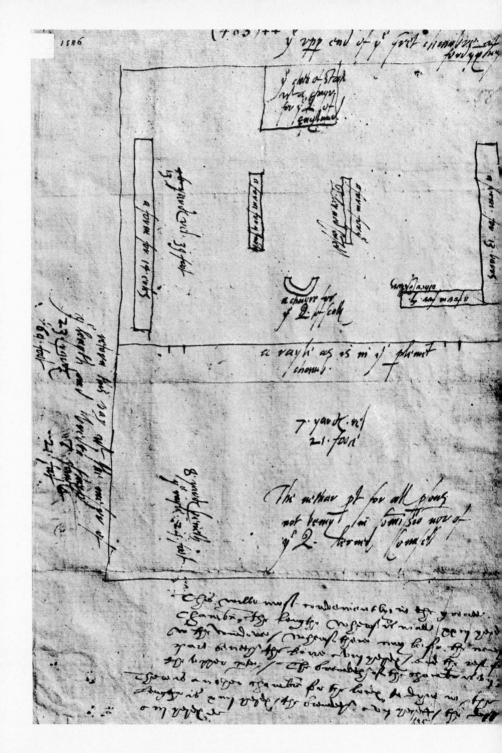

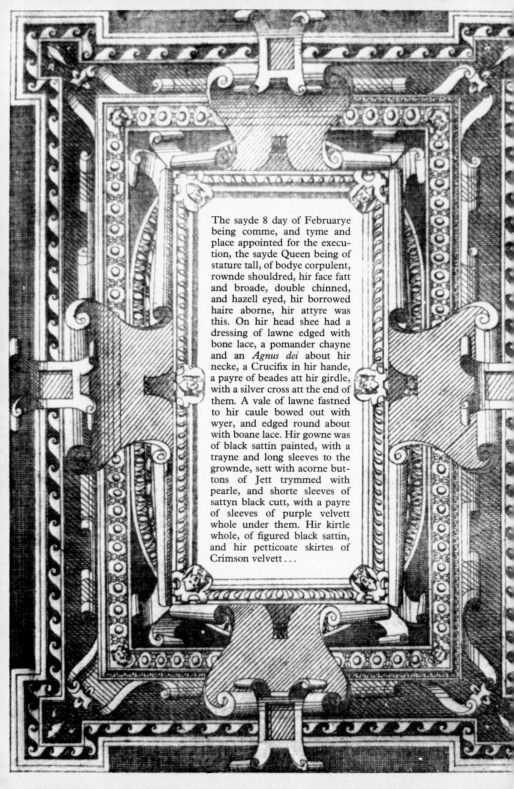

The sayde 8 day of Februarye being comme, and tyme and place appointed for the execution, the sayde Queen being of stature tall, of bodye corpulent, rownde shouldred, hir face fatt and broade, double chinned, and hazell eyed, hir borrowed haire aborne, hir attyre was this. On hir head shee had a dressing of lawne edged with bone lace, a pomander chayne and an *Agnus dei* about hir necke, a Crucifix in hir hande, a payre of beades att hir girdle, with a silver cross att the end of them. A vale of lawne fastned to hir caule bowed out with wyer, and edged round about with boane lace. Hir gowne was of black sattin painted, with a trayne and long sleeves to the grownde, sett with acorne buttons of Jett trymmed with pearle, and shorte sleeves of sattyn black cutt, with a payre of sleeves of purple velvett whole under them. Hir kirtle whole, of figured black sattin, and hir petticoate skirtes of Crimson velvett . . .

Then, with an unappalled countenance, without any terror of the place, the persons, or the preparacions, she camme out of the entrye into the hall, stept upp to the Scaffold, being two foot high and twelve foot broade, with rayles rownde about, hanged and covered with black, with a lowe stoole, longe fayre cushion, and a block covered also with black. The stoole brought hir, shee sat down. . . . the queen satt upon hir stoole, having hir *Agnus Dei*, crucifixe, beades, and an office in Lattyn. Thus furnished . . . shee began verie fastly with teares and a lowde voice to praye in Lattin, and in the middst of hir prayers, with overmuch weeping and mourning, slipt of hir stoole, and kneeling presently sayde divers other Lattin prayers . . .

Then she began to kiss hir crucifix, and to cross hir self, saying these wordes, 'Even as thy armes, oh, Jesu Christ, were spredd heer upon the cross, so receive me into the armes of mercye.' Then the two executioners kneeled downe unto hir, desiring hir to forgive them hir death. Shee answered, 'I forgive yow with all my harte. For I hope this death shall give an end to all my troubles.' They, with hir two weomen helping, began to disroabe hir.

During the disroabing of this queen, shee never altred hir countenance, but smiling sayde shee never had such groomes before to make hir unreadye, nor ever did putt of hir cloathes before such a companye. At lengthe unattyred and un- apparelled to hir petticoate and kirtle, the two weomen burst out into a great and pittiful shrieking, crying, and lamenta- tion, crossed themselve, and prayed in Lattine. The queen turned towardes them: *'Ne cry vous, j'ay preye pur vous'* : and so crossed and kissed them, and bad them praye for hir.

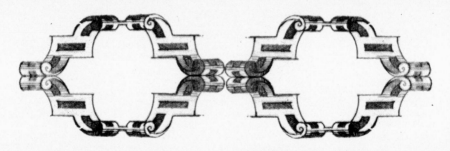

One of the weomen having a Corpus Christi cloathe, lapped it upp three corner wise, and kissed it, and put it over the face of hir queen, and pynned it fast upon the caule of hir head. Then the two weomen departed. The queen kneeled downe upon the cushion resolutely, and, without any token of feare of deathe, sayde allowde in Lattin the psalme, *In te, domine, confido*. Then groaping for the block, shee layde down hir head, putting hir chain over hir backe with bothe hir handes, which, holding their still, had been cut off, had they not been espyed.

Then she layde hir self upon the blocke most quietly, and stretching out hir armes and legges cryed out: *In manus tuas, domine, commendo spiritum meum*, three or four tymes.

Att last, while one of the Executioners held hir streightly with one of his handes, the other gave two stroakes with an Axe before he did cutt of hir head, and yet lefte a little grissle behinde.

Shee made very smale noyse, no part stirred from the place where shee laye. The Executioners lifted upp the head, and bad God save the Queen. Then hir dressinge of Lawne fell from hir head, which appeared as graye as if shee had byn thre score and ten yeares olde powled very short. Hir face much altred, hir lips stirred upp and downe almost a quarter of an hower after hir head was cut off. Then sayde Mr. Deane: 'So perish all the Queen's ennemyes.'

MARIE STEWART REYNE DE FRAN ET DESCOSSE

Et les belles beätez, et les grandeur plus grandes,
Sont pleines de dangers, et de Malheurs diuers:
Ce sont Buttes a Maux: Qui n'en croira mes vers
Viene voir ceste Reyne, et life ses legendes.

Tho. de leu F. et ex.

Alive a Quene, now dead I am a Sainte;
   Once Mary calld, my name nowe
      Martyr is;
From earthly raigne debarred by restraint,
   In liew whereof I raigne in heavenly
      blisse.

My life my greife, my death hath wrought my
      joye,
   My frendes my foyle, my foes my weale
      procur'd;
My speedy death hath shortned longe annoye,
   And losse of life an endles life assur'd.

AN INVENTARYE OF THE JEWELLS PLATE MONEY AND OTHER GOODS FOUND IN THE CUSTODY OF THE SEVERAL SERVANTS OF THE LATE QUENE OF SCOTTES

Furniture for a bedd wrought with needle woorke silke, silver and golde, with divers devices and armes, not throughlie finished.

A clothe of Estate garnished with armes.

A little tablet of gold enameled, containinge the picture of the Kinge of Scottes.

A little bottell of gold contayninge a stone medicinable for the collicke.

A great Agnus Dei, with a glasse of christall sett in ebene woodd.

A little tree of gold, with a Queen sitting in the tope and a boy pulling down the branches.

A little gold bodekin to stick in a woman's hear with a saphir at the end.

A little crown of thornes in gold enameled with a white saphir at the end.

The sayd late Queen's owne trenchar, of silver gilt.

A little silver candlestick, which served to hange at the sayd Queen's beddes head.

A gown of russett damask furred with gray coney.

An old black velvet gown, broken.

All her stockens.

All her gloves.

Eight payre of sheetes, which served for the sayd Queen's own bedd.

Fyve dozen of smockes.

A payre of perfumed gloves.

A watche.

All her confitures, succattes, preserves, conserves and other medicinable drugges.

The chayre wherein she was woont to be caryed, covered with velvet.

Sowing silk and rawe silk of all colours.

A clothe of State of brown crimsen velvet embrodered with a single trewe love knott.

In looking upon her cloth of estate, I noted this sentence embroidered, 'En ma fin est mon commencement', which is a riddle I understand not.

The decline of Mary's physical appearance was related to the breakdown
her health after her arrival in England. Shrewsbury wrote to Cecil in
rch 1569 that for a fortnight the Queen had done nothing but complain
he spleen 'wherewith oft times, by reason of great pains through windy
tter amending unto her head and other parts, she is ready to swoon'.
hough she stage-managed her health in attempts to secure improve-
nts in her living conditions and movement from one house to another,
ry was without doubt an ailing woman. Suffering from lack of exercise
he open air and chilled by the cold of draughty north-country manor-
ses, she became a martyr to rheumatic gout and dropsy. Periodic visits,
dgingly granted, to take the waters at Buxton, close to Bess of Hard-
k's estate at Chatsworth, eased the pain but never cured her. By 1581 the
llings were so bad that she was moved around by her servants in a litter.
ter after letter written by gaolers tell of long periods, weeks running
months, when she never stirred from her bed or from her chamber,
pled with agonising rheumatic pain in her hands, side and leg. We catch
hetic glimpses of her being carried out in a chair by her servants into the
den or placed by the edge of a duckpond to watch a hunt. Occasionally
carriage ambled its way along the roads of the Shrewsbury estate
ring the commodious figure of the prematurely aged Queen.

ile she had been Queen of France and Queen of Scotland she had
ssed magnificently. Chronicles and inventories list the splendours of
dresses, nearly all of cloth of gold and silver, velvet, satin or silk. Then
re were a hundred and thirty-one items in her wardrobe, including sixty
vns and fourteen cloaks. The clothes of exile reflect the sombre image of
portraits. These were of black, white, grey and violet, colours of widow-
d, trimmed with jet or simple passement braids. In 1586 she had
rteen robes, thirteen mantes or *manteau*, thirteen vasquines or petti-
ts, fifteen *pourpoincts* and five juppes. Many were described as *vieux*.
ss demanded occasion and there were none for a Queen who made no

public appearances and whose every movement was to be concealed fr
the outside world. The simple, almost gaunt, costume she chose dramati
her situation as she gradually cast herself over the years into the rôle of
martyr Queen. Black softened by diaphanous veils was flattering to a fig
whose proportions gradually expanded over the years, and it enhanced
attributes of crucifix and rosary. A tailor was part of her household a
Mary possessed a genuine interest in fashion. Even after almost a decade
imprisonment she was still able to write gaily to her agent in Paris asking
the latest fashions at the French court and giving orders that an artifi
make her two headdresses with crowns of gold and silver 'such as t
formerly made for me'. Another was charged to search even farther af
for the newest modes from Italy 'in headdresses, and veils, and ribbons'.

The jewels of exile were also few. When she had left France she returi
not only with the Scottish crown jewels, but with those bestowed on
during her years at the Valois court. In 1562 these numbered some hund:
and eighty items, including the celebrated Great Harry, a vast pendant
with a huge diamond and a ruby, her mother's grand diamond cross
chain enriched with rubies and diamonds, and seven jewels so rich
diamonds that she willed them as ornaments for the Queens of Scotla
Most of the jewels she left behind when she fled from Edinburgh Ca:
and some of them, including her celebrated black pearls, were unsc
pulously sold by Regent Murray to Elizabeth I. In contrast to such mag
ficence the jewel inventories of exile make sad reading. One tells of a mir
of ebony, a jewel like a tree of gold with a lady sitting in its branch
another also like a tree but in which nestled two parrots, jewels agai
poison and an oval stone set in gold 'against melancholy'. When she v
seized at Chartley and committed for trial not only were her papers tal
but some of her possessions stolen. This time there is mention of a look
glass containing miniatures of Mary and Elizabeth, enamelled and g
nished with diamonds, a chest set with diamonds, rubies and pea
bracelets of agate, a pin case of gold at the end of a waist chain besides ot
jewels. Even her wardrobe was rudely ransacked and two doublets, a pai
silk stockings, three embroidered scarfs and a black velvet hat with gr
and white feathers were taken.

'ithin the enclosed court of the Queen of Scots the days slowly came
\d went. At eleven o'clock each day the great gates were shut for an hour
hile the household dined. Of Mary it was reported in 1581 that 'she eats
\it little, and drinks more, but not immoderately'. She had her own cook,
ho for a period acted also as her apothecary, and sixteen dishes, sometimes
\ore and sometimes less, were prepared each day for the royal household.
he Queen always lived in fear of being poisoned and therefore wrote to
rance for a piece of unicorn's horn as an antidote. Such an object must
\ve been sent, for it is recorded laying by her bedside at Chartley and
:er at Fotheringhay; in her will she left it to her son. Into the cups and
shes which she consumed her servants ceremonially plunged the unicorn.
Meals punctuated the rhythm of a day only rarely interrupted by any
\ppening of consequence. Occasionally a visitor from France appeared to
scuss her dower lands, or there would be some other event to celebrate,
·r observance of the Royal Maundy, or her standing godmother to one of
e Shrewsbury grandchildren. The work of her gaolers was to deprive her
all means of contact with the outside world, to keep her as an unwelcome
rvivor from another era who should be allowed to live out the charade of
·r royalty but to see that it was acted out before an unappreciative
\dience and preferably none at all. Mary was an ardent letter-writer and
e more she was cut off from the world, the more obsessive her corres-
•ndence became. Enormous quantities of time must have been spent in
cret conclave with her secretaries and ladies establishing ways and means
maintaining contact with the world which lay outside. From the house-
\ld of forty surrounding her spread out the network of communications,
ostly by way of lowly people, a tutor, a glover, a musician or a bookseller.
hese ventured their lives in order that the Queen of Scots might write to
e King of Spain or her agent in Paris or enter into the bewildering net
intrigue such as might lead to her release. The system was always
·eaking down, always subject to sudden discovery and endless dislocation.
; she was moved from place to place and plot succeeded plot her miniature
\urt was forever having to recreate its contacts. Over the years Mary
\adually therefore became an adept at secret handwriting and at codes.
'he best and most secret writing,' she counsels, 'is with alum dissolved in

a very little clear water twenty four hours before you wish to write and
read it it is necessary only to dip the paper into a basin of clear water; tl
secret writing appears white, very easily read until the paper becomes d
again; you can in this way write on white taffata, or white cloth, especial
lawn.' The cost of maintaining such secret channels was often conceal
in the bills for gold and silver thread for her needlework.

Embroidery she shared as a passion with her keeper's wife, La
Shrewsbury. Like her dress and her letter-writing, this too was a means
demonstrating her plight through her choice of allegory and symbol. I
this means she could express enigmatically what she dare not write
words. The embroideries of Mary Queen of Scots are silent letters
posterity in handwriting of rainbow silks and metallic thread telling of t
misfortunes of a martyred Queen. In her will she left a magnificent bed
her son embroidered by herself in silk, silver and gold with coats of ar
and emblematic devices. William Drummond of Hawthornden describ
them in a letter to Ben Jonson, the poet. Across the curtains the you
King of Scots could read an edited version of his mother's history. I
could see the devices of the kings of France and of members of the house
Lorraine, from whom he was descended and to whom he was related. I
could study his mother as she depicted herself in the midst of a tissue
allegory, appropriately kneeling at the foot of a crucifix. Other panels we
more cryptic in their symbolic import. On one there were two wom
astride the wheel of Fortune, one holding a lance, the other a cornucop
with the motto, *Fortunae Comites*, the companions of Fortune, alluding
her rival the Queen of England. Mary depicted herself as a bird in a ca
with a hawk poised menacingly above, or as a wheel plunging downwar
into the sea beneath *Senza Speranza*, or as the sun in eclipse. Hours m
have been passed compiling programmes for these hangings, studyi
books full of curious emblems and devices, or choosing pictures of stran
beasts from Gesner's *History of Animals* with which to fill up the vaca
velvet between. In the surviving examples of her embroidery at Oxbur
Hall and Hardwick the mythology burgeons. Once again she gives vist
voice to her attitude to Elizabeth: a monogram, made up of both Quee

mes, bears the defiant motto *The bonds of virtue are straiter than of ood*, while above a tree of golden apples, of the sort awarded by Paris to e most beautiful of the goddesses, there runs *Be it given to the fairer*.

Over the years vast areas of fabric must have been covered by the ueen and Lady Shrewsbury as they sat in a circle with their attendant dies working over the tablecloths, cushions and hangings listed in their ventories. Every item was scattered with arms and emblems, every piece rinkled with gold and silver spangles to catch the light. Occasionally ch work was done as gifts. Mary embroidered a cushion with her own vice of a hand cutting down vines and the motto *Virtue flourisheth by a und* for her suitor, the Duke of Norfolk. From time to time there were mpaigns to pacify the Queen of England, whose hands readily received e petticoats and nightdresses worked by her cousin. Occasionally such esents met with a rude rebuff. Her son, King James VI, sent back his other's embroidered vest as she had sent it addressed to the Prince of cotland.

Mary's day was essentially static. Once, long ago in childhood, she had ily voyaged *en fête* from one French royal château to the next along the ire valley or made progress to the remoter regions of her Scottish mains. Now she was moved only as necessity demanded, necessity being litical for fear of escape, domestic for the cleansing of her rooms or edicinal for the taking of hot springs at Buxton. Whether she rode on rse-back or in her carriage her movements were always to be kept un- nounced and unheralded. Surrounded by guards the Queen and her urt were silently moved from one house to another, or hurried through a wn warned against making any form of demonstration. Shrewsbury ice wrote: 'I have not suffered the simplest of them for seven years to alk abroad, nor stir out of doors, except with an armed guard.' For the bjects of the Queen of England the Queen of Scots might just as well not ve existed in their midst. For fourteen out of her seventeen years in ison she moved from one end of Lord Shrewsbury's vast park to the her as she was lodged alternately at Sheffield Castle or Sheffield Lodge. he discovery of each plot to rescue her resulted in ever closer confine-

ment. For long periods members of the Queen's court were not allowe
beyond the boundary of the great gate of the house, and Mary herse
would remain in her chambers taking air by pacing along the leads of th
roof each day for an hour. Later this would be extended to perambulatio
indoors in Lord Shrewsbury's great dining-room and walks in the cour
yard. Mary, attended by Lady Shrewsbury, with their attendant ladi
following at a respectful distance, daily processed in this manner. Althoug
possessed of a passion for the chase, this exercise was mostly denied h
for fear of an escape. Occasionally the restriction was rescinded and sh
was allowed to take part in the hunt so that she might see the actions of
favourite bloodhound. Her last hunt was deliberately stage-managed whi
her rooms were ransacked for evidence of her complicity in the Babingt
Plot.

In her youth she had loved all outdoor exercises. She shot at the butt
played golf and croquet and hunted. Now her consolation lay for the mo
part in expeditions to the gardens and waters surrounding the gre
houses to which she was confined. Her delight was in animals, little dog
spaniels and bloodhounds, turtle-doves and barbary-fowls, and all kin
of pretty caged birds. Her letters tell of their arrival from France or of the
presentation to friends. These creatures freely gave her the love an
affection which life was sharply to deny her. Her little dog crept onto th
scaffold and lay immovable between the severed head and the body of h
mistress.

As the years passed religion increasingly brought its consolation in ac
of devotion and piety. It is reflected in the jewels of exile, in the golde
crosses and huge rosaries she wore, in the *Agnus Dei* of rock crystal er
graved with the Passion, and in the Book of Hours written with her ow
hand. Over the years religious exercises gained in momentum. Norfolk
execution threw her into 'great contemplation, fasting and prayer'. In 157
she paints a pen-picture of the devotions of her household. Devoid of

est, they gathered daily for the reading of a sermon in French. She ites that she is concerned lest the rumour be true that the Pope had ·bidden the use of the vernacular tongue for prayer. Although the glish government denied her the services of a priest, by 1584 one was rt of her household. He was a Frenchman, Camille de Préau: officially scribed as her almoner or reader, he was a priest in disguise. Sir Amias ulet describes him dressed 'in court-like suit, a brooch in his hat, silver ttons, his garments of all colours'. Twice a day the Queen's household embled in her dining-room to hear him read to them, sometimes in tin, spies ominously reported. Although his presence was denied her on : scaffold he makes an odd appearance in her funeral procession wearing ong gown and bearing a silver cross making his way towards Peter-rough Cathedral. One catches the conventionality of Mary's piety in r meditations on adversity and in her poems:

> O Lord, my God, do Thou this prayer receive,
>   As I submit me to Thy Holy Will;
> And, while my soul to this sad earth shall cleave,
>   O grant me power to yield in patience still!

Mary was passionately loyal to friends and to her personal servants. ais is reflected in her last hours with her little household, each one of 1om was lovingly remembered. As a woman she was, however, greatly ren to tempestuous emotions. Her gaolers write of her 'stormy manner d threatenings' and, unlike her cousin of England, she readily broke wn into floods of tears. She possessed enormous personal charm when e chose to exert it, aided by a voice described by contemporaries as soft d alluring. In her youth she sang well, and even at the end of her life lutes ebony and ivory are recorded as being in her possession. As she grew ler the Queen gave way to melancholic periods of deep introspection, but r manner in her youth is recorded as being lively, affable, frank even to

excess. Although never a woman of deep learning she had had the educ
tion of a renaissance princess at the most cultivated court in Europe. Sh
spoke and wrote French, Italian and Scottish with ease, and over the yea
attained a working knowledge of English. Throughout her life she su
tained a love of French poetry, which in fact she wrote, and Ronsard h.
for a time been part of her court. Even in her imprisonment he remember‹
and dedicated a volume of his verses to her. She loved romances and hac
passion for history, wherewith she was once moved to remark that t
chronicles of England were notable for their shedding of blood.

Throughout her life Mary remained essentially, both in outlook and
intellect, a Frenchwoman. Her behaviour was always conditioned by h
upbringing and she thought of government and policy in terms of t
personal intrigues and *amours* which motivated politics at the Valois cou
Both in Scotland and in England such an outlook was to have disastro
consequences.

Mary Stuart's day gradually drew to its close in the same way that it h;
opened. A drum roll at six in the evening in winter and eight in summ
announced the oncome of night. Once more the great gates were shut ar
the two households turned in on themselves. Guards armed at all poin
took up their positions at the entrances to the royal apartments with
which Mary and her shadow court supped and passed the evenin
Shrewsbury wrote that 'it is one of the clock every night ere she go to bec
so assiduous was she in the care she exercised over the members of h
household. Mary never slept on her own and in a nearby bed lay a lady-ii
waiting; by her own bed-head stood a solitary candle to lighten her dar
ness. After seventeen years of such an existence the terrible announceme
that there were to be no more days must have come to Mary Stuart as
blessed relief. It was like the opening of a door through which she wou
pass, away from this life of unremitting boredom, of immovable mela
choly, of trying to keep up appearances, of sad little pleasures gained on
suddenly to be withheld. It was an end to a living death for a Queen wl
had once moved upon the stage of history as one of its most brilliant ar
controversial figures.

Inventory of Spectacles and Evocations

HE CHILD QUEEN

rawing by François Clouet, 1552

*Iary Queen of Scots in her ninth year, a
·awing by Clouet probably made for her
·ture mother-in-law, Catherine de' Medici.
·our years before, Mary's grandmother,
·ntoinette de Bourbon, had described her as
·lere brune . . . car le taint est beau et cler et
· chair blanche, le bas du vysage bien jolly,
·s yeux sont petis et ung petit enfoncé le
·sage ung petit long'.*

· and 11

HE PALACES AND GARDENS
F CHILDHOOD

*Iary grew up with the children of Henry II,
·aring their education and round of court
·e. Her earliest memories were of the palaces
·d châteaux of the French crown, Blois,
·net, Fontainebleau and Amboise. Through-
·t her life Mary remained in her tastes
· Frenchwoman. She maintained French
·ople in her service, even into captivity,
·rmally conversed and wrote in French,
·re French court dress and read French
·erature.*

·2

UEEN-DAUPHINESS

·iniature by François Clouet, c. 1560

Iary at about the age of eighteen.

·3

UEEN OF ENGLAND

·ndant jewel bearing the arms of Mary
·ueen of Scots

Translation of a Latin verse celebrating
Mary as Queen of England used in a
pageant at Tournelles

*On 17th November 1558 Mary I of England
died. Henry II of France caused his daughter-
in-law to be proclaimed Queen of England,
Scotland and Ireland. Court poets celebrated
the expansion of the French monarchy to
include the British Isles, and the arms of
England quartering those of France were
used in all court fêtes, on the Queen's plate
and on her seals. Elizabeth I was never to
forgive the Queen of Scots for this defiant
gesture against her succession to the crown of
England.*

14 and 15

QUEEN OF FRANCE

Drawing by François Clouet, c. 1560

Brantôme describes the Queen.

16 and 17

A ROYAL JEWEL

Pendant jewel bearing a cameo of Mary
Queen of Scots, c. 1565

*A number of cameo jewels of Mary survive.
In this jewel the likeness of the Queen of
Scots has been mounted into a locket of
enamelled gold set with rubies and diamonds.*

18 and 19

QUEEN OF SCOTS

Brantôme describes Mary wearing Scottish
costume

The garb of a Scotswoman from *Recueil de
la Diversité des Habits*, 1562

THE WIDOW

20 Portrait by an unknown artist after François Clouet, c. 1560

21 Drawing by François Clouet, c. 1560

On 22nd August 1560 Sir Nicholas Throckmorton, the English ambassador in Paris, reported Mary's intention of sending her portrait to Queen Elizabeth: 'Quoth she, "I perceive you like me better when I look sadly than when I look merrily, for it is told me that you desired to have me pictured when I wore the deuil."' White was the traditional colour of mourning for the Queens of France and Mary wore it twice, once in 1559 on the death of her father-in-law, Henry II, and a second time on the death of her husband, Francis II, in December 1560.

22

ROYAL COINS AND MEDALS

Medal struck to commemorate her marriage to the Dauphin Francis, 1558

Silver testoon (enlarged) struck by Achesoun, 1553

Medal struck to commemorate her marriage to Henry Stuart, Lord Darnley, 1565

23

HOLYROODHOUSE IN 1561

Items from the inventory of furniture in Holyroodhouse in November 1561. This list gives a very vivid impression of Mary's surroundings during the years of her rule in Scotland when she deliberately attempted to create a life about herself based on the pattern of the French court. A hundred and eighty-six items are listed, including ten cloths of estate, forty-five beds, twenty-three sets of tapestry, eighty-one cushions, two folding stools, twenty-four linen tablecloths and a

litter. A few of these items can be traced in lists of her possessions in captivity: a cloth of estate embroidered with the arms of Scotland and Lorraine and a set of tapestries depicting the victory of Gaston de Foix at the battle of Ravenna in 1512. The latter adorned Mary's rooms both at Chartley and Fotheringhay.

24

MARY WEARING A BONNET

Painting by an unknown artist after portrait of c. 1560–65

Mary was painted more at this time of her life than at any other. In 1561 she presented her picture to Elizabeth I and the two queens exchanged portraits again the year after. When Sir James Melville visited the English court in 1564 Elizabeth showed him a miniature of Mary which she kept in a cabinet in her bedroom.

25

THE POETESS

Sonnet of Mary Queen of Scots to Elizabeth I, 1568

This elegant sonnet in Italian was written by Mary to persuade Elizabeth to grant her a personal interview. In translation it reads as follows:

> A longing haunts my spirit day and night
> Bitter and sweet, torments my aching heart
> Between doubt and fear, it holds its wayward part,
> And while it lingers, rest and peace take flight.
>
> Dear sister, if these lines too boldly speak
> Of my fond wish to see you, 'tis for this –
> That I repine and sink in bitterness,
> If still denied the favour that I seek.
>
> I have seen a ship freed from control
> On the high seas, outside a friendly port,
> And what was peaceful change to woe and pain;
> Even so am I, a lonely, trembling soul,
> Fearing – not you, but to be made the sport
> Of Fate, that bursts the closest, strongest chain.

ary loved poetry and poets, all of whom
d paid tribute to her at the French court
h eulogies of her beauty and accomplish-
nts. Brantôme records having seen the
een both in France and in Scotland read-
poetry with tears and sighs from the
art. This sonnet to Elizabeth I was com-
sed in both French and Italian to urge that
y should meet, an event which was never to
pen. Mary demonstrated her love for
thwell in a passionate sonnet sequence,
ich was used as evidence to demonstrate
complicity in Darnley's murder.

HE QUEEN'S LIBRARY

ventory of the Queen's books in Edin-
rgh Castle, 26th March 1578.

selection of books from the inventory of
ary's library which she left behind in her
ht from Edinburgh Castle. This was kept
ring her reign in a room in Holyroodhouse
peted with green cloth and was catalogued
three parts devoted to Greek, Latin and
dern languages. Most of the two hundred
d forty books were brought by Mary from
ance and they reflect her passion for
tory and for French poetry. Brantôme
ords that she reserved two hours a day to
dy and read, and that after her return to
otland she read Livy every day after
ner under the guidance of her future
amer, the humanist, George Buchanan.

JEEN OF SCOTLAND

graving attributed to Frans Huys, c.
59

28 and 29

KING AND QUEEN OF SCOTS

Portrait by an unknown artist, c. 1565 (?)

*Mary married Henry Stuart, Lord Darnley
on 29th July 1565. This is the only contemporary painting depicting them as husband and wife.*

30 and 31

THE QUEEN'S WARDROBE

Inventory of the royal wardrobe at Holyroodhouse, February 1562.

*Items from the one hundred and thirty-one
entries listed in the wardrobe of her dresses
early in 1562. Sixty gowns are described,
nearly all of cloth of gold, cloth of silver,
velvet, satin and silk, fourteen cloaks, seven
of which were of Spanish cut, thirty-four
vasquines or petticoats and sixteen devants or
stomachers. The list includes robes for the
deuil and costumes for court masquerades.*

32 and 33

THE QUEEN'S JEWELS

Inventory of the Queen's Jewels, August
1561

The Penicuik Jewels: earring, necklace
and locket traditionally owned by Mary
Queen of Scots

*Mary Queen of Scots' jewels were a source of
great interest to her contemporaries. After
the death of Francis II in December 1560 she
returned to her mother-in-law all the French
royal jewels, but she carried back to Scotland
with her those items by right the property of
Queens' Dowager besides those belonging to
the Scottish crown. She returned to her
kingdom with a hundred and fifty-nine pieces
in all, forty-three of which were kept within
her own private cabinet. Later she showered*

them on Bothwell and subsequently entrusted their safekeeping to Murray who sold, amongst other things, Mary's celebrated black pearls to Elizabeth I. When she finally fled Edinburgh she left nearly all her jewels behind. In England she had few and the sad list includes a number of jewels effective against poison and an oval stone in gold 'against melancholy'.

34
THE QUEEN'S FACE

Mary's complexion was fresh and clear but not brilliant. Sir James Melville wrote that 'the Queen of England was whytter, but our Queen was very lusome'. Her eyes were sparkling hazel or dark grey. Due to her bad health and the conditions of her imprisonment her beauty swiftly declined. At twenty-seven Shrewsbury could write of her, 'Truly her colour and complexion of her face is presently much decayed,' while an observer at her trial in 1586 brutally describes her face as 'full and flat, double chinned, and hasel eyed'.

35
THE QUEEN'S HANDS

Brantôme describes Mary's beautiful white hands displayed to perfection when playing the lute. In her attempt to escape from Lochleven Castle, her exquisite hands betrayed her true identity. Disguised as a laundress she revealed her hands accidentally while trying to prevent the boatman from lowering the muffler which concealed her face.

36
THE QUEEN'S HAIR

Miniature from the Book of Hours of Catherine de' Medici c. 1573

Nicholas White to Sir William Cecil, 1569

Mary's hair seems to have changed its natur colour progressively during the first twen years of her life from a ruddy yellow auburn, from auburn to dark brown black, finally turning grey long before time. Brantôme describes it as 'si beaux, blonds et cendrez' but on the scaffold s wore an auburn wig concealing her own he 'polled very short'. Mary was fortunate having in her service Mary Seton whom t susceptible White describes as 'the fine dresser of a woman's hair that is to be seen any country' and relates how the Que appeared every day with 'a new device head dressing'.

37
THE FACE OF THE IMPRISONED QUEEN

Painting by an unknown artist based or miniature by Nicholas Hilliard of 1578

38 and 39
EMBLEMS OF A CAPTIVE QUEE

Drawings of emblems on a watch of Mary Queen of Scots, 1576

Letter of William Drummond of Ha' thornden to Ben Jonson describing a b embroidered by Mary Queen of Sco 1616

Emblematic panels from the Oxbur; bedhangings embroidered by Mary Que of Scots, c. 1570

The renaissance passion for emblems enabl Mary Queen of Scots covertly to express h dilemma and her attitudes more forcefu than she ever dared in words. This she did her embroideries and, apparently, in jew. lery such as the emblematic watch who symbols were carefully copied by the Engl government early in 1576. Many emble. recur in both embroideries and jewellery : o

th an eclipse of the sun and moon seems to
er to her relationship with Elizabeth I.
r own personal emblem or 'impresa' was a
nd clasping a sickle pruning a vine and the
tto: Virescit vulnere virtus (Virtue
urisheth by a wound).

)

ARY AT THE AGE OF
)RTY-SIX

iniature by Nicholas Hilliard, 1578 (?)

holas White to Sir William Cecil,
bruary 1569

e most important likeness of Mary Queen
Scots painted during her captivity and the
rce for the great full-lengths manufactured
her son's reign (see no. 41). Nicholas
lliard was Elizabeth's miniaturist and the
eliness of the characterisation makes it
tually certain that he must have been
mitted to paint her from life.

HE KING'S MOTHER

rtrait by an unknown artist, c. 1610

the accession of Mary's son, James VI, as
ing of England in 1603 there arose a
mand for pictures of his mother. These
re painted in the fashionable idiom of the
cobean age, full length, the figure standing
a Turkey carpet with a shiny silk curtain
ped behind. Several examples of these
sthumous portraits exist, including the
st famous of them all, the one reproduced
re, the so-called Oudry Portrait.

OTHER AND CHILD

ood engraving from John Leslie's De
gine, Moribus gestis Scotorum, 1578

rtrait by an unknown artist, 1583

After Mary fled to England she never saw her
son again and his education was put into the
hands of Mary's arch-defamer, George
Buchanan. Mary never, however, recognised
the reality of James's attitude towards her
and to the end she retained maternal feelings
for him.

43

THE QUEEN WRITES TO HER GODCHILD

Letter to Bess Pierrepoint, September 1583

Bess Pierrepoint was one of Bess of Hardwick's grandchildren and one of Mary's
godchildren. She remained in the service of
Mary until 1586, when the Queen's secretary
Nau fell in love with her, leading to her
departure from the household.

44 and 45

THE QUEEN'S EMBROIDERY

Panels from the Oxburgh bedhangings
embroidered by Mary Queen of Scots, the
Countess of Shrewsbury and attendant
ladies, c. 1570

Nicholas White to Sir William Cecil,
February 1569

Cushion cover embroidered by Mary
Queen of Scots

Mary embroidered throughout her life but
above all during the period of her captivity.
She and Lady Shrewsbury passed long parts
of the day with the needle surrounded by
attendant ladies seated on stools. Mary's
interest in embroidery was intense. While in
Lochleven Castle she had petitioned for 'an
imbroider to draw forthe such work as she
would be occupied about'. Mary had a
succession of embroiderers, including Pierre
Oudry and Charles Plouvart, whose task was
to aid the Queen by drawing patterns and
supervising the mounting of the finished
panels onto velvet.

The Oxburgh bedhangings, one of which is dated *1570*, were planned and designed by Mary Queen of Scots in conjunction with Bess of Hardwick. They consist of panels of velvet onto which have been stitched panels bearing emblems and animals copied from Gesner's Icones Animalium, *1562*. Apart from these there are two cushions by her at Hardwick Hall.

46

THE QUEEN'S ANIMALS

Mary to the Archbishop of Glasgow, 1574

Mary's passion for animals is reflected even in the subject matter of her jewels. While she reigned in Scotland two loaves a day were provided for dogs and there are payments for 'blue velvet for collars to the Queen's little dogs'. Birds and dogs were a constant source of delight to her during her confinement and her little dog followed her to the scaffold, lying down between the severed head and the corpse until forcibly removed and washed clean of the Queen's blood.

47

PORTRAIT OF A PRISONER

Miniature by an unknown artist, *c.* 1575–80

Mary to the Archbishop of Glasgow, 1575

Mary had great difficulty in obtaining portraits of herself to distribute to loyal friends and it seems she had them manufactured in France and smuggled over.

48 and 49

THE MAKING OF A MARTYR

Verses written in a Book of Hours, 1579 (?)

Items from an inventory of Mary's poss‹ sions at Chartley, 1586

As the years of captivity passed the Que‹ gradually assumed a piety not noticeable her youth. Exile, ill health, her role as ‹ Catholic claimant to the English throne, a the denial to her of the practice of her fai‹ all contributed to a growing preoccupati‹ with the religious life. This is reflected occasional pious poems, in the Essay Adversity, *composed in 1580, and in ‹ daily round of the life of her household w‹ its regular meetings for readings and praye‹*

50 and 51

THE QUEEN'S TRIAL

Plan of the trial

Drawing of the Great Chamber at Fothe‹ inghay with the trial

Mary's fate was sealed by her involvement the Babington Conspiracy, the last of t‹ long series of plots against Elizabeth centring on the Queen of Scots. On 8‹ August 1586 she was moved from Chart‹ into solitary confinement at Tixall a‹ finally, on 25th September, moved to t‹ castle of Fotheringhay. Here on 14th a‹ 15th October she was brought to tri‹ sentence of death being finally passed‹ Westminster on 25th October.
The plan and view tally closely: dominati‹ the whole scene was the empty chair of st‹ representing the absent Queen of Engla‹ opposite to which there is the chair in whi‹ the Queen of Scots sat (not indicated in t‹ view). The two queens were divided by ‹ table or tables at which sat the justices a‹ the Queen's counsel.

HE QUEEN GOES TO HER EATH

etter of Robert Wyngfield to Lord urghley

Iary was executed on the morning of 8th ebruary 1587 at Fotheringhay Castle. She as informed of her execution on the evening fore by the Earls of Shrewsbury and Kent. hey denied her the services of a priest and ld her that Elizabeth had also declined her quest to be buried in France. Mary spent r last evening amongst her attendants, stributing small items of remembrance and oviding in other ways for the dissolution of r household. She then prepared herself to e as a martyr for the Catholic faith. It was tween eight and nine in the morning when e was finally summoned to the Great Hall.

obert Wyngfield's letter to Burghley gives e most detailed eye-witness account of her d. The description was needed by Burghley hen he prepared the official English account her death. No one connected with her usehold was allowed to leave England until e government's narrative of what had ansacted had been broadcast. When mem- rs of her household reached France further tails of her end became available.

HE QUEEN ATTIRED FOR HER XECUTION

inting by an unknown artist

his portrait was commissioned by Elizabeth urle who, together with Jane Kennedy, tended Mary on the scaffold. Elizabeth was e sister of Mary's secretary, Gilbert Curle, o, after the execution, withdrew to Ant- rp. In her will of 1620 she left this picture

to the Scottish College at Douai : 'je laisse ... un grand portrait de sa Majestée vetu comme Elle etoit à son martyre.' The portrait is clearly posthumous, probably painted c. 1610–15, but executed under careful super- vision to record the Queen's appearance on 8th February 1587. Elizabeth Curle and Jane Kennedy can be seen weeping in the background to the right.

54 and 55

THE QUEEN ON THE SCAFFOLD

Letter of Robert Wyngfield to Lord Burghley

Drawing of the Great Hall at Fotheringhay with the execution

The drawing, which is preserved amongst the papers of Robert Beale, Clerk of the Council and the man who carried the death-warrant to Fotheringhay, depicts the lay-out and incidents in the execution. The Queen enters at the top left attended by her women and preceded by the sheriff of the county. She is next seen being disrobed on the scaffold by Jane Kennedy and Elizabeth Curle with the Earls of Shrewsbury and Kent seated to the left, while the Dean of Peterborough, whose ministrations she declined, stands below. At the top right of the scaffold the executioner is seen about to strike. Standing in a row at the back of the hall, numbered 7, are the four men of her household who were allowed to attend her : Robert Melville, 'her poticary, surgeon and one other old man besides'.

56 and 57

THE BEHEADING

Letter of Robert Wyngfield to Lord Burghley

THE ACT AND THE AFTERMATH

After the execution Mary's household was confined until the official government version of what had happened had been published to the courts of Europe. The block and every other item, blood-stained or otherwise, connected with the execution was scrubbed clean or burnt for fear of becoming relics.

QUEEN DOWAGER OF FRANCE

Engraving by Thomas de Leu

An engraving issued in France showing Mary late in life wearing mourning robes of a type normally associated with those adopted by her mother-in-law, Catherine de' Medici.

THE MARTYRED QUEEN

Engraving by an unknown artist

Poem by Robert Southwell

Almost immediately after her death, Mary was transmuted by her followers into a saint in the Catholic cause. In Paris the news of her execution evoked mass demonstrations and sermons dilating upon her bravery and on the sanctity of her end.

THE QUEEN'S CHATTELS

A selection of items left by the Queen after her death. Mary left instructions for the division of her household and personal effects amongst her servants and for the sale of certain items, such as her coach, by Melville and her physicians to pay for the journey of her servants homewards.

FILIAL PIETY

Tomb by Cornelius and William Cur
c. 1606–1616

On 30th July 1587 Mary was finally buri in Peterborough Cathedral after a delay over five months. The service was a Pr testant one, although Mary's servants d walk in the actual funeral procession. On accession in 1603 her son, James I, under t influence of Henry Howard, Earl of Nort ampton, erected the tomb in Westminst Abbey. Mary's body was moved to its la resting-place in 1612.

EPILOGUE

Reverse of a locket bearing relics Catholic martyrs and a miniature of Ma Queen of Scots

Robert White to Sir William Cecil, Febr ary 1569

The motto on her cloth of estate was that her mother, Mary of Lorraine.

Image Index

All items listed below are portraits of Mary Queen of Scots unless otherwise stated. For the iconography of the Queen the reader is referred to Roy Strong, *Tudor and Jacobean Portraits*, London, 1969.

The Royal Collection, reproduced by gracious permission of Her Majesty The Queen: miniature by François Clouet (12, 30, 35).

The Duke of Atholl: double portrait with James VI (31, 32, 35, 42); D. Bower Collection, Chiddingstone Castle, Kent (49); Bibliothèque Nationale, Paris: drawing by François Clouet (14, 32, 34), the 'Deuil Blanc' by François Clouet (21), miniature with Francis II from the Book of Hours of Catherine de' Medici (36); British Museum: coins and medals (22); Beale MSS: View of trial (23, 51), View of execution (54, 55); Musée Condé, Chantilly: drawing by François Clouet (9, 32, 34); National Museum of Antiquities of Scotland: pendant jewel (13), pendant jewel with cameo of Mary Queen of Scots (16, 17), the Penicuik Jewels (33); National Portrait Galley, London: no. 1766 (24, 30, 31, 32), no. 429 (31, 32, 34, 37); National Trust, Hardwick Hall: double portrait with Lord Darnley (28, 23, 29, 30), the 'Oudry' portrait (23, 41); private collection: miniature by Nicholas Hilliard (40); Public Record Office, London: poem to Elizabeth I (25), emblems from a watch of Mary Queen of Scots (38); St Mary's College, Blair, Aberdeenshire: memorial portrait (49, 56), memorial locket (64); Scottish National Portrait Gallery: no. 186 (20, 31, 34), no. 1073 (31, 35), no. 1217 (58).

Contemporary engravings of the Queen and borders and decorations from late sixteenth-century French books.

ACKNOWLEDGEMENTS

The authors wish to thank Mr John McKendry and the staff of the Department of Prints and Photographs, Metropolitan Museum of Art, New York. They also wish to thank Sally Harvey for her assistance in preparing the book for the press.